Aster(ix) Journal
www.asterixjournal.com

Editor-in-chief/Founder
Angie Cruz

Publisher/Founder
Adriana E. Ramírez

Managing Editor
Tanya Shirazi

Editorial Assistants
Clarissa León
Joshua Graber
Katherinna Mar

Book Review Editor
Lucia LoTempio

Contributing Editors
Rosa Alcalá, Arielle Greenberg, Yona Harvey, Daisy Hernandez, J. A. Howard, Sheila Maldonado, Dawn Lundy Martin, Oindrila Mukherjee, Idra Novey, Emily Raboteau, Nelly Rosario, Zohra Saed, Sun Yung Shin, Jenelle Troxell, Chika Unigwe, Marta Lucía Vargas, Autumn Womack, Elleni Centime Zeleke

Advisory Editors
Ari Ariel, Armando Garcia, Amy Sara Carroll, Norma Cantú, Xochi Candalaria, Jennifer Clement, Edwidge Danticat, Cristina García, Stephanie Elizondo Griest, Andrea Thome, Helena Maria Viramontes

Aster(ix) print issues are usually published 2-3 times a year in print with additional content online. **Aster(ix)** is funded in part by the Dietrich School of Arts and Sciences and the Department of English at University of Pittsburgh.

More Aster(ix) Anthologies

Inheritance
Summer 2019

(Un)bound
Winter 2018/2019

Edges
Fall 2018

Dirty Laundry
Fall 2017

Kitchen Table Translation
Summer 2017

Best of Kweli
Spring 2017

What We Love
Fall 2016

Atravesando
Spring 2016

available for order wherever books are sold

Aster(ix) Journal

presents

The Poetry Issue

Winter 2020

✳ ✳ ✳

Edited and Curated by
Amy Sara Carroll,
Saretta Morgan, &
Marta Lucía Vargas

BLUE SKETCH PRESS | PITTSBURGH

Published via Blue Sketch Press, Pittsburgh.
www.bluesketchpress.com

The Poetry Issue
An Aster(ix) Anthology / Aster(ix) Journal
Edited by Amy Sara Carroll, Saretta Morgan, & Marta Lucía Vargas—1st ed.
          ISBN (print)   978-1-942547-12-9 (trade paperback)
                                    1-942547-12-9 (ISBN-10)
Cover art by Youmna Chlala
Cover Design by Little Owl Creative.
Copy-Edited by Joseph N. Welch III.

First Edition: February 2020

Printed in the United States of America
9 8 7 6 5 4 3 2 1

Thank you to all the Aster(ix) familia who helped us solicit and select work for this issue and also to everyone who showed up on May 4th 2019 to Angie's apartment in Washington Heights to begin what we hope will be an ongoing series of editorial events inspired by the conceptual and scholarly work of Jenelle Troxell on little magazines: Rosa Alcalá, Arielle Greenberg, Ayanna Mathis, Dawn Lundy Martin, Saretta Morgan, Oindrila Mukherjee, Emily Raboteau, Zohra Saed, Chika Unigwe and Elleni Centime Zeleke.

Contents

A Conversation with Poets

The Editors

[The following is a selection of email responses from the poets in this issue to a series of question we sent to each.]

This special issue of Aster(ix) has evolved. When Angie, Marta, Saretta and Jenelle brought us together, the plan was to solicit work in a variety of forms—per Jane Heap and Margaret Anderson's unique modernist aesthetics (inseparable from the pair's collaborative editorial method). Everything more or less went according to plan (sans, regrettably, Heap and Anderson's signature swinging divan), but, in a curious twist of fate, our attentions became concentrated in the poetic. To put it bluntly, this issue has become all poetry. One hypothesis—a provocation— to explain our focus: The issue has become all poetry in the early twenty-first century because the absorptive genre has retained and fine-tuned its capacity to assume the shape of any and all other genres with which it comes in contact. Thoughts? Affirmations? Repudiations?

Vidhu Aggarwal: At various points, I have made a temporary move away from poetry in favor of other genres such as science fiction, but I keep coming back to poetry as a pivot into mediums such as pulp fiction, Bollywood movies, and video games. My own poetics practice involves multi-media combos, such as visual collage, video, photography, and performance. I have also collaborated with graphic artists, choreographers, and sound artists in making poems. The very permeability of poetry allows me to settle, if only briefly, into these alternative spaces. Lately I've been meditating on poetic forms as "clouds" that can grow, dissipate, descend, ascend, penetrate, be penetrated, be digital, be deus ex machina, be epic, be lyric, be archive, be monstrous, be almost transparent. The mobility of poetry is a stealth trick in an atmospheric package. Think of Wordsworth's lyric, lonely wandering in a dispersed, ephemeral cloud unit. In conceptualizing a "cloud poetics," I've been reading Tung-Hui Hu's book *The Prehistory of the Cloud*, an examination of the metaphor of the "cloud" for the networked, amorphous, decentered spaces for our online activities, archives, and ghostly footprints. How does the poem function as an expanding, dissipating, non-sovereign, intra-penetrable archive? What enters and exits a poem over time? "Locust Formation," a poem I started many years ago, has undergone numerous permutations, begun as an approach to Martha Graham's choreography, and may evolve into other vaporous transformations.

Raquel Gutiérrez: Poetry is taking me to a space of alliteration as my proclivity for poetry lies in its porous promiscuity. It's possibility to spill my truth in all of its slippage right off the page. Poetry is a performance. It's not like I can push my hand through the space-time continuum and meet the histories I speak of that help and hinder my ability to fully avow my shadow. And yet poetry might be where it does something that looks like the ignition of a history otherwise left dormant in the libraries we don't frequent enough or the JSTOR vaults we can't access. The absorptive genre, poetry is the pill.

Global attention to the movements of people and goods (and the

consequences of those movements) is crucial to understanding how we exercise power in our own lives. If you were to think of your poem as a map, what are the economies and/or geographies (cosmological, terrestrial, subterranean, etc) that it connects?

VA: "Locust Formation" is part of a manuscript *Daughter Isotope* that maps out coordinates between ancient and contemporary cosmologies, which speaks to my own gaps in knowledge across various U.S. and South Asian cultural archives. As a 1.5 generation immigrant, I access the fantasy space of India and the U.S. through multiple, disparate "texts." "Locust Formation" interacts with a line from the Rig Veda that describes the beginning of the world as "seven half-embryos portion out the semen of the world at Vishnu's command" (translated by Wendy Doniger). To me, this cosmic command animates a series of strange militaristic dance formations that ultimately decenter male desire, and go rogue—as in a biblical plague of "It Girls." In "Locust Formation," I attempt to address economies of desire though evoking generations of women whose presence on the world stage conceals/reveals gendered violence, whether mythological (say, Draupadi from the epic Mahabharata) or historical—the millions of women who have responded to the #metoo hashtag.

최 **Lindsay (LC):** The work has its roots in a historical investment in the source material, which is coming from early 20th-century Korea, during the Japanese colonial occupation—specifically 1936, about 21 years after the start of the occupation and just short of a decade before the end. The historical problem that I think about in Heliotrope isn't as explicitly stated in the excerpt published in this journal, but it takes shape around the Japanese colonial government's policy regarding leprosy—the short of it is that the Japanese government selected an island off the southeastern coast of the peninsula to convert into a national leprosium, and evicted all of the original occupants. The government enforced a strict quarantine policy in Korea, such that by the 1940s, over 6,000 Koreans with leprosy were incarcerated on this island, called Sorokdo. Various accounts by people who were quarantined on Sorokdo testify that the colony was the site of forced sterilization, medical experimentation, torture, and enslavement, as the incarcerated lepers were forced to labor toward the Japanese war effort without pay. People were forcibly quarantined on Sorokdo until 1963, and the island has been accessible to outsiders only since 2007. The work I'm doing is trying to trace the threads of this history and the problems of historiography. In attempt to be brief—if this poem were a map, it would be invested in tracing the lines that flow between Korea, America, and Japan, primarily, though there seems to be no containment within a world-system, and across a long swath of time with a particular intensity knotted around the early 20th-Century to the present. And it would be invested in the interplay between pathology, religion, and colonial power, which leads to many times and places. But it would probably have to be a map with an arrow pointing to a dot at the exact space and time where I am, with a bubble saying: "You are here"—I doubt my ability to make a map of this poem—at best, I imagine I'm standing with a compass, writing an attempt to find orientation.

Aldrin Valdez:: If this poem were a map it would trace the migration of families from the Philippine archipelago to the U.S.

It would show flights from Manila to Anchorage to New York City. That is how my siblings and I got to JFK International Airport, finally being reunited with our parents after eight years apart. Remittances are critical to the economy and they come from all over the world. My parents had come to work in NY in the mid-to-late 80s in order to provide for family back home. Our reunion, however, also separated us from my grandmother in Manila. My last day in the Philippines was the last day I saw her. A map of migration can provide context for a person's loneliness and fear of abandonment. It would show what happens to family photographs and letters that survive their writers.

Elisabeth Frost and Dianne Kornberg: These works address the mass extinctions that are underway due to human desecration of the environment, including man-made global warming. In this way, a "map" of economies in "Remains" primarily would include vectors or relationships among human and nonhuman animals. The geographies vary, but the two pieces here both refer to ocean habitats. The time span referenced over the course of the full series ranges from seconds to millennia.

Jamie Gray Gillette: "Drive safe" emerges from a pictorial vision of American pastoral geography, one historically imagined and produced by landscape paintings of the Industrial Revolution and environmentalist writers like John Muir (wherein nature is a geography of leisure, separate from labor, a symbol of white national identity). The poem takes place on Interstate 95 heading North out of Philadelphia, towards New York, but it attempts to challenge the utopian visions of the traveling poem genre a la Whitman's "Song of the Open Road." The WANTED billboard springs from an economy of fear, splicing the barn/cattle/sunrise with its mega-size production, its garish proclamation of danger and evil. The lobster dinner exists in a space of nostalgia and domesticity, born from my own coastal New England background. Just as violence is woven into the picturesque tradition of the land the poem traverses, the consumptive tradition of the lobster dinner is also laced with assault and carnage. The image of milk poured into eyes is, finally, connected to a geography of resistance, drawn from photographs of pepper sprayed protestors during the 2015 Baltimore protests for

Freddie Gray. The substances of blood and oil (in the margin of the road), and milk, remain to evidence the violence that produced them.

RG: This poem traffics in celestial geographies as it is from where the reader can see the vicissitudes of violences that have ravaged the land, the concept, and its attending material landscapes. A poem speeds up and slows down time, finding points in history's spectrum and its false linearities, for a reader to imagine by their own method for image—realist or abstract—the series of skirmishes and massacres that metabolize in memory. The poem is divining ancestral memory.

Christina Olivares: (Economy of memory) Global memory or personal memory: her body an organ along which befores-and-afters travel. What does a good ———— in the americas want? Of touching her face, her hair. Of wearing her. Of wearying her. Of leaving her everywhere I go. An economy of language communicating, among other confusions, silences. Geography, terrestrial: everything I can know is this body I inhabit. Many bloods, many earths, but not all of them. Temporary, energetic.

(A child's cosmology) Tarmac. Bus route. Calle Jovellar. Heath Avenue. 193rd and Bainbridge. All the terrestrial that permeates skin.

(If a map) I'd draw a line from the Bronx to Havana to New Orleans to Santiago de Cuba to Guantanamo. End in the ocean, which I draw as us. Or I ask us all to stand together, all the children in my generation in my family, as children, with our hands open. I match up the routes in our palms side-by-size like puzzles. When they get wet with rain or tears or spit or blood or syrup, wetness rivulets between us.

Alternately, or additionally, describe your writing space/s. (Hint: at the close of Chapter 6 of Borderlands/La Frontera: The New Mestiza, Gloria Anzaldúa describes the altar above her desk.) We're talking literal space/s here.

Kimberly Alidio: Activated, humming boundaries; some tolerance for an autonomy that looks like loss of so-called status and opportunity; tourmaline, black kyanite, obsidian; access to emotional info; the Nap Ministry IG; a raised eyebrow at the literary star system, hustler culture, normative arts institutions, academia.

LC: I usually write at my desk, in my apartment in Berkeley. I live in a studio, and from my window I can see the screen covering the metal hull at the back end of the Berkeley Art Museum and Pacific Film Archive; I often write very early in the morning, around 4 or 5 a.m.—before sunrise—and I remember that for a time, in the early days of working on this manuscript, I would look out the window to see the glow of the screen briefly glinting against and coloring the morning rain. Every time the image on the screen changed, all of the drops would seem alight with color, for a moment so brief you could imagine that you'd imagined it—like pixels, falling through the air. I loved the quiet and the privacy of the phenomenon—that it was so ephemeral I could imagine that there was at once no possibility of sharing it with anyone, and grace from the closure of impossibility. Above my desk, I have a poster of Simone Weil's mugshot which I took from a Danish magazine I stumbled across in Copenhagen, and a print of the first two stanzas of §3 of "I. Remembering Into Sleep," a part of Rosmarie Waldrop's long poem The Ambition of Ghosts.

I've also written parts of this project in the English graduate library at UC Berkeley, several cafes in the East Bay, Assistens Cemetery in

Nørrebro, Stockholm, and a bit in New York—I tend to work in notes, for a long period of time, until I feel a need to write, so much of the work happens in transit, until I need to sit and be quiet for hours.

AV: I write on the subway on my phone. Or on this laptop in my room when I can stay emotionally present long enough. My journal/sketchbook is a hybrid space, more immediate and full of crossouts, a space for drawings and collage that obscure & articulate, become part of the writing and vice versa. Text and texture.

Dianne Kornberg: My studio has been an 800 square foot building that my husband and I built on an isolated outer island in the San Juan archipelago in Washington State. It's been a peaceful place to work with few interruptions, and provided space for making large works. Since I moved to a ferry-served island, my workspace is more restrictive and I have scaled down the size of my prints. The biggest obstacle to our collaboration is that we live on opposite coasts of the country. Elisabeth visits my studio annually, and otherwise we work via email and phone.

Elisabeth Frost: My desk is a massive, apparently DIY wood creation, which I found in the basement of the apartment building where I live. My previous desk was a battleship gray clunker, which I bought for $25 and a pizza in Pennsylvania. I held onto it for almost 20 years because I didn't feel entitled to purchase something I actually loved. I am grateful that this gigantic wood desk found me. In terms of our collaboration, I have been thrilled to work often in Dianne's studio. I have learned from her persistence and tenacity as an artist with a dedication to her practice that has been a gift to me. The time that we share in her space is crucial to our process.

JGG: The carrel desk assigned to me in the Bard College library, for the purposes of writing my senior thesis, is pressed up against the carrel desk of another student: a squash player from Turkey, who is double majoring in literature and economics. Ever squeamish about the threat of someone spying on my works-in-progress, I initially recoiled from the idea of keeping my writing space in such close company. I've made a habit of writing alone, occupying a comfortable rhythm of producing and unveiling, producing and unveiling, a rhythm that relies on the strict demarcation between a private creative space and the products of that space deemed acceptable for other ears/eyes. If my neighbor shared these feelings, he didn't let on. Most days when I arrive at our desks, he pulls his head from Finance Capitalism and its Discontents to ask me how my writing is going. Sometimes, in his rare absence, he leaves me a book (the latest, a collection of Nabokov's short stories, with a sticky note listing his favorites). I recently left him In the Heart of the Heart of the Country by William Gass as thanks, and he returned it within a few days, having already finished most of it. Much like our shelves of books that lean against each other, we share our respective generative spaces with generosity and quiet collaborativity. Sometimes, as we sit side-by-side typing away at our projects, it feels as though we are co-creating, breeding kinetic energy between us, helping the other gain momentum. My relationship with my desk-mate is transforming the way I think about the function of a creative community: not just as a round table of people to whom you can bring polished drafts, but as an ongoing conversation, which of course requires more uncertainty, humility, and vulnerability than the model of producing and unveiling, but in turn forms circuits that allow creative electricity to transmute, and spark.

RG: I have a not-terrible Ikea knotty pine workshop-style table in the kitchen nook with a photograph of the kiosk you encounter when you arrive to Slab City near the Salton Sea. "Almost There" is crudely spraypainted on the kiosk which helps me feel like I might soon arrive to my destination even if that destination is a site of chaos. Do I want to get there? That's the anxiety that animates my writing. Within that nook space there's light from a big window and on its sill I have photographs of family from my childhood, postcards from Monument Valley, feminist art buttons, art flyers that speak to a life engaged with a world outside. Writing is where these vectors come together.

CO: My grandmother bought me a kitchen table and four wavering chairs from a furniture store uptown about a decade ago. I'd left town for a month to work, and when I returned I found she—worried that I'd lived there for a year without a proper table—had used my spare key and secretly deployed my aunt to place her gift in my living room. The table is a dark brown color that releases stain when wet. I've fed so many people I love on it, and it's seen everything I've written since 2009. I also write on the train for an hour plus on my way to work, though hardly ever on the way home: my favorite seat is to the immediate left of the center door, and I work on my phone or in a notebook and put my bag at my feet between my legs. I rarely use the desk in my bedroom, a soft raw pine that still smells like earth, selected for writing but stacked with books.

In the 1980s, Lone Justice sang, "Nobody knows about inspiration." Tell us about yours.

LC: The project I'm currently working on started to develop when I became aware of an already present obsession with a poem by modernist Korean poet 서정주 (Seo Jung-Joo), called "문둥이" ("The Leper"). I think I encountered it for the first time during my freshman year in college—around 2014, maybe—and it took until the summer of 2018 to realize the psychic space it was taking in my life. By the time I'd noticed that this was something I'd been doing, I'd spent years translating the poem, over and over again, nearly every day and often multiple times a day, on various scraps of paper and my academic notebooks, intentionally playing with it and distorting it as I tried to understand what it was about the poem that fascinated me—and as I tried to understand the poem. I was at the Kundiman retreat that summer, and thinking about the relationship between poetry and research in my life, and my orientations towards and within both of these things—this is when I decided to begin to take up the work of this fascination intentionally, and the threads began to weave together.

In terms of textual inspirations and influences—I was thinking about "compromised translation," having just co-edited and released a journal of collaborations and, in some cases, deliberately "distorted" translations between Swedish and American poets. This work was inspiring to me. And I was thinking particularly about Anna Moschovakis's "compromised translation" in her poem, "Flat White (20/20)," in They and We Will Get Into Trouble For This, as well as Sawako Nakayasu's Mouth: Eats Color. As the process has gone on, more and more inspirations have accreted—many of them are directly cited in the work, but some more subterranean influences are coming from the Nag Hammadi Library, and from the practice of exegetical commentary in Alexandrian literature—Origen's commentaries on the Gospel of John and on the Song of Songs are particularly beautiful examples.

EF/DK: In our collaborative work, we have developed ideas that have led each of us into new territory. The challenge for Dianne has primarily been incorporating text into images in such a way that the words become a visual element in the work, as well as having verbal meaning. For Elisabeth, the work has not only helped sustain a creative practice but also led to completely new material and approaches—most broadly, the natural world as subject, and often with specific reference to the tools of collectors, botanists, and marine biologists.

JGG: An incomplete list: lobsters and their exoskeletons (specifically their ritual of shedding, in which the lobster builds a copy of her exoskeleton inside her current shell, then ruptures the membrane between carapace and abdomen and crawls out of herself); a photo album of my mom age twenty through forty, that I keep by my bed; "Aubade: Some Peaches, After Storm," a poem by Carl Phillips, that I keep at my desk; a few new books of poetry: *A Sand Book* by Ariana Reines; *Ghost Of* by Diana Khoi Ngyuen; *Sight Lines* by Arthur Sze; an older book of poetry: *Lunch Poems* by Frank O'Hara; images of the island where I grew up (the shore that fringes into docks along Narragansett Bay to receive quahogging dinghys and ferries of tourists); stores of water, oceans, bays, reservoirs, estuaries, floodplains; photographic archives of memory and the personal mythologies that photographs enable us to build, the materials with which we fabricate our self-narrative (see: album of mom age twenty through forty); and the acts of circuitous disassembly and reincarnation of the body in nature that destabilize these narratives of the singular, linear self (see: the lobster continually giving birth to herself, then eating the shell she just escaped for calcium, constantly reallocating the materials of her skeleton to form and reform her body).

RG: The impulse to defend oneself. How institutions convince you that you need them to produce knowledge. The way a group of people might be called together to participate willingly in the shared experience of grief. Walking. The young people of Chile and Lebanon.

This poem/work is in conversation with whom, with what?

LC: I've been thinking often of this passage in Walter Benjamin's *The Arcades Project*—it's in Convolute N, [N2a, 3]:

> It's not that what is past casts its light on what is present, or what is present its light on what is past; rather, image is that wherein what-has-been comes together in a flash with the now to form a constellation. In other words, image is dialectics at a standstill. For while the relation of the present to the past is a purely temporal, continuous one, the relation of what-has-been to the now is dialectical: is not progression but image, suddenly emergent. Only dialectical images are genuine images (that is, not archaic); and the place where one encounters them is language. []Awakening[]

Much of the project takes place in and out of increasingly distorted translation, and the rest I've started to think of, in shorthand, as a practice of citation and commentary. While I usually say in the body of the project who and what I'm in conversation with, it's too many to say, and probably includes many people and things I'm not aware of. *The Arcades Project* is one text I don't cite very frequently, though it's been a presiding spirit. The other is a fragment of Ludwig Wittgenstein—"How small a thought it takes to fill a whole life."

AV: One conversation is with Anne Carson's *Autobiography of Red*. I borrow a line from the beginning of the book: "latches of being".

EF/DK: *Remains* is a series of sixteen paired images and texts that are in conversation with one another, as we were in producing the work. As in most of our other series, *Remains* engages with visual and verbal idioms of specimen collection and preservation, while also challenging the assumptions and conventions of some Western scientific methods. We were concerned with "remains" on both the individual and the species level. What is left, post-mortem? And what will "remain" (survive) in the Anthropocene? Each pairing evolved differently, but in the two pieces included here, the image inspired the text. The tubeworm's mineral remains prompted a text that explores humans' contamination of the planet's oceans. The humor and the almost Baroque lines found in the image of a skate (aka a "mermaid's purse") led to a more playful piece about gender, embodiment, and sexuality.

KA: Poets who write poems that know things and care little for whatever in poetry and the world distracts and detracts from that knowing's essentially autonomous power.

Speaking of literal space/s, in your praxis, how do poems occupy pages? How do poems interact with images, grow into themselves as images?

AV: I think of the page as a field. How and where I position the text, how I shape it, is connected to the breath and pace I want the writing to have, and to the imagistic quality of words, lines, and stanzas. I want it to feel and look good, look right. As in: OK, this poem needs to float away from the left, closer to the right. It belongs right there.

EF/DK: Because visual language and poetic language "read" so differently, some argue that verbal language incorporated in or adjacent to visual art limits the visual experience by limiting an open-ended visual interpretation of the work. As we have collaborated to create numerous text/image series over the past decade, we have challenged this idea, considering image and text alike not just as inter-dependent but also as "legible" in two ways: as abstraction and as symbolic content. *Remains* is unlike most of our projects because the text is not visually incorporated into the image itself. In this regard it is more traditional, or more bound by the "rules" of visual image vs. poetic text as separate entities. As we move forward, we may or may not make more work in this mode.

JGG: I like the possibilities for metaphor between the mechanics of the skeletal system and the operative form of a poem. A beautiful example of a form that feels functional, that produces meaning in and of itself, happens in Ngyuen's *Ghost Of*, in which she writes in and around the shape.

RG: Aren't poems just images rendered with care and reverence? Or rather that's what they are for me. The poem is the frame, the saturation, the subtext, the rainwater barrel in a thunderstorm, a collector of textures, inhaling and exhaling. The poem is a site responsive performance of the image. The poem helps reveal the way the image might constellate with nature, violence, aggression, bravery, history, witness, philosophy, ideology, space and affect.

CO: I aim for -- relational and electric -- in the poems. If I fuss at them long enough, usually something catches. They talk to each other. I write groups (books) of poems at the same time and only rarely independent poems one at a time. They arise in me as if they have kinship networks. An image starts here and ends over there or not at all. Also I'm working on not privileging images over other forms of sensory perception, including the near-sensory somethings of premonition and intuition, and memory, forgetting, wanting.

A question that you wish someone would ask you. An answer for that question.

AV: "How do we heal centuries of colonial damage?" I don't have an answer that solves or fixes the damage, but the image that comes to my mind in response to the question, is of foreheads touching. I want someone to ask the question as a way to begin an unraveling of silences. And maybe as we speak, there is also silence as a necessary space for however our bodies need to move.

bowerbird

Aldrin Valdez

Still want to trouble color
names as latches of
being. In the photograph
of my mind: her ash-gray
face under the glass and
jasmine garlands. A gray
that is almost lavender.
Everything else is
chiffon-white & glossed.
She says in her letter
there is pain in her side.
She hopes to get better
soon. In the decades
since, the ink has seeped
into the paper, has
purpled its fibers.

Sequence from
Botanic América

Christina Olivares

sparrows void sneaker hollows
thrown over a telephone line
with nests. at dusk

we are little, crowded
in a backseat, dirt-funky and
playing the quiet

game. we break when we spy
mcdonald's, glow singing us singing
back as a lady in front wavers high

high high: it's always apocalypsing.
apocalypso: riddled earthbody tilts

as it sprouts us, in this

home-land a homeland to us

our américa, an

unpracticed parent
unparalleled lover

(later: her body as mine,

shock of a love: discovering there was this growing thing in us both)

like   the burning a body does when it is touched
        the burning a home does when it is torched

exhibit a: the land which can be done upon and to
exhibit b: a series of encounters with desire
exhibit c: language

tell me in how many words
do you come from?

a love song to a place
        a place that is queer

a love song to a place of queerness

           a love song to queers

                a love song to the queers I love

I speak in unfamiliar languages

none mine

        ausente como

are we imaginable?

what do   we
                 our
                 these
                         children imagine?

That summer I dreamt a pony at the door
and I woke up
                         my small awed hands poking

in the dusked light squared
                         above and so eagerly

wishing for the being I dreamed.
                         I check, breathless,
                         all ripe want. For me. Also for us.

No pony:

what's a pony to a girlchild in the projects?
a regurgitated dream?
a fever-dream of your best girl self?
beautiful, hot to the touch,
unoriginal?   can you
be good enough for one
to appear for you—first you, then
the dream of the queer animal you are
afraid to be, such good,
good girls both?

I say the Bronx burned—

        what I am sure of is
        we ate its earth as children: a transfer of desiring.

        silky-threaded little bodies plus
        burned land's milky sustaining
        coding and becoming in us
        a redressed burning—a desire in it as us
        to be ever more and more embodied,
        redolent   a burned earth resituated
        and made new again in our
        little new bodies, a

queer love song:

different américa built itself inside of us, a botanical
no-américa, inverse that survived,   made new

américa   home land.
If a child   consumes dirt, what new does the child become?
Children   of the américas eat earth because they are hungry:
farce of scarcity.   Different kinds of hunger.   Our knowledges
are also loosely archived,   tightly archived, hidden away,

oh américa,   a fever
dream edging delight   an archive of grief thickly
                                              renders us
                            we remember ourselves
vaguely,

        as if we and not this are/is the dream of   américa.

First

Christina Olivares

I discovered myself first: needling towards blank pleasure,
my hands where they weren't supposed to be, curled

towards what'd been hidden from me. I came
and coming learned my name: *take me home, take me home, take me.*

Nobody ever caught me. Nobody ever said, direct, *you can't love girls
like you.* But I knew. Overspilled and luscious, how disgraceful:

slough this body. Mock it clean. Lop it, lick it, prune it clean. Sinuous,
vestigial bluff of a body, contempt flowered this body

wet with fear, wet with shame, every cell wet. A whole condition
that only alchemizes into freedom if you don't die from it

first. I know to be embodied in each or any américa
is to be ruined by violence, and wow how many forms does its violence

take. The second person I ever loved taught me delight:

lay me in a bordered plot of field and when she saw me naked, marveled,
whispered into my ear as her hands found me: *You are just like me.*

Was I? A split seed, she took root in my tongue.

No Se Fue Nada: Somos La Luz

Christina Olivares

These islands were once not islands but a contiguous stretch of earth
lifted from what's called Venezuela to what's called Cuba and

when the sea rose later, drifting and curling and drowning
the lowest parts, all that was left was sea moving between these

fashioned places with older names. People learned to row, mapping
a blue body where they had mapped a dry body before on foot.

Salt water thins and thrums strangely in the blood. So too we know
a hibiscus flower, flor de jamaica, salt and blood and meat of codfish.
We know

how to turn a half-rot platano sweet in the pan. Who knows how to fix
a thing
intent on breaking: islands threaded with thready infrastructure and
populated

inches above a now-boiling sea. Stolen power makes everybody sick for
generations. Pathology of this sort of theft is something about allowing
oneself

to become unsure about what qualifies a person to be a person.
It is not enough I am a person if you believe you have the power to decide

otherwise. *Whiteness* is one word for that pathology. Another: it is not
a mistake that *zombie*
connotes terror inflicted by the macoutes. A person becomes a zombie when

the pathology of stolen power takes root and festers, and a person is for sure a zombie
when they believe they get to decide who's a person and who's not a person

and serve that verdict with violence. It is of note that what brings a zombie back
is salt. Imagine a salted sea rising. What does it take for us to become

the salted sea rising, to nibble at the land between us, teach us to row
towards each other? I wonder how to transform my body into something useful:

an electrical grid, perhaps. A dry wind and plaster. Something to hold homes
in place. Oxygen, antibiotics. Organs beating cool in a cool box, a doctor's hands.

I imagine this body part-of, not parceled. Useful, not compromised.
I imagine it compromised and useful and fractured and belonging to something

we haven't invented new language to name yet. Perhaps there will be never be

consensus on what we are. Perhaps *we* is a fiction.

Oyá sings to me from her graveyard, her hands full of keys:

You've already lost if you believe you're powerless. Take what little land is remaindered

in any space your body occupies—the nation is complex in us—and fashion a home.

Say a truthful thing. Carry the words inside of you and give birth to them at inopportune

times. Clean out its eyes, burn the killing thing that took root.

What is tourism but facing a drowning sea and pretending
it isn't filled with blood. Histories sing strangely. The noisiest ghosts
populate memory.

Maybe there is no power tonight. Se fue la luz. But how brilliant if you can imagine
all eyes are tonight, in this blanketing night,

somos la luz, la luz prendida, we are our own lamplight, la luz encendida.

Us Versus Us

Raquel Gutiérrez

I drive all night | Oakland to Tucson | I am a Texas Eagle | Sunset Limited
| I am 14 hours of fisting fury to find | our Barrio Anita bohemian
hideaway | hurrying a longhorn skull summons over threshold | A mid-
life high speed chase | to take back what we lost in the treaty | to say ours,
a re-encounter, could endure | a broken down swamp cooler | Another
Southern Pacific dust storm | and then another one at the end | here
come the trains | June has us wearing our skins again | your bush is the
biggest I have ever seen |We get along trying Nina Simone on my phone
| prying her out of these full-throated speakers | My white t-shirt makes
you gasp goddamn suavecito | Tom Waits on Vicente then more Nina
on vinyl | (even the record player sweats) | An upcoming neighborhood
| Where if I left the bed I could see | railroad tracks adjacent | where the
money worth one man | who steals 19 heads of cattle | the fact Camp
Grant Massacres[1] us in the mood | It put us Mexicans against us Indians
us versus us | sus tierras verdaderas | The Airbnb omits that Eskiminzin
had a reputation | as the leader of a nation before blood became rational
| he smelt fear among whites | we deal fear against whites | Sam Hughes
cared about his health when he moved to Southern Arizona | as the
quarrel and war | father of a neighborhood you find beneath you | and
you beneath me | I almost bled through my seersucker pants and boat

---

shoes | as the hungry coyotes approve our hunt | and our eyes locked the first time you turn me onto Lana Del Rey | and her libertarian lullabies | like all of this was a good idea | You can take me anywhere | I meant to say with | Apache tears for all | your daddy, a master narrative | a red star, gray curls | saturnine and scent-free | who left her baby in my charms | a mercy killing with a job talk, an epigraph | a monument in the making | a walk into the feral waters of the river's side, California | no stones in her pocket | she could barely touch the deep | and here your body takes vengeance | takes shelter | for onward we lover in captivity | and take back what we lost in the treaty | Our bodies, our landscapes— our bodies are landscapes | We ate dinner at a place called A Little Thing | where the owner shell-gamed our fucking | and looked down at our tattoos | I brought out my crystals | the accessories to conjure | give us strength, forgive our sins, Eskiminzin[2] | who shared an evening meal with McKinney | and upon their conclusion | the two smoked a cigarette together | a cherry brightened dusk | ready to receive any man who stands in line for him | For any coward can kill his enemy | it takes a brave man to kill his friend

---

2   Eskiminzin was a high ranking member of the Aravaipa Apaches, a chief who lost two wives and six children in the massacre.

Redacted from History

Raquel Gutiérrez

Tú. Eres la testiga
a mi entrega.

Staring out a 10th floor window onto a city
I could never afford to be from again

In downtown LA, I find shelter in your chest.

From mouthfucking on Monday night,
to the penultimate look you gave me Saturday
morning, as the haze in the early- May
sky begins to lift. We had to return to
the places that house our traces.

Have you ever been alienated by your labor?

Your body pressed against and
behind me; your breasts sashay to meet
the swagger in the small of my back,
Your breath on my neck; as your mouth cruises

the boulevard of my earlobes.

Ay, 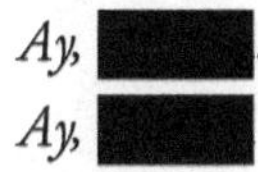 .
Ay,

And your name, a record
made illegible
in its intended Castellano

Drive safe

Jamie Gray Gillette

There is oil in the margin of the road
And blood.

There is a barn that will not hold
Under the snow.

And there, the cattle who know
the weight that is coming for them.

Here, is a pot full of water.

Here, is the heat at the seam of the lid.

Here, are his hands around the thorax of a lobster.
Here, a dish of lemon and butter.

There he is WANTED on the billboard.
There is his neck, pink with sunrise.

There is the milk he borrowed,
There is his neighbor, her body swollen like a sentence.

There are the women
Pouring milk into their eyes,
And just beyond his neck
The sun is rising out of Philadelphia.

From the series *Remains*

Elisabeth Frost and Dianne Kornberg

Accessory of a siren, horny case, skate egg pouch—what might come out of a mermaid's purse? Cell phone and lipstick? Lover's kinky scat? Or a living ray? If washed up at the strand line, only crisp brown remains. Flat round clutch. Arabesque for a strap. One-time incipience, wanna-be juvenile—oh baby, baby.

49

In afterlife the collagen went rogue, fossilized
into a maze of mineral hollows, curves of du-
plexes bequeathed to no one. Once, flesh un-
folded in little rings, each added on like a first-
grade sum, its body storing our contaminants.

ELISABETH FROST AND DIANNE KORNBERG

excerpt from *Heliotrope*

최 Lindsay

According to Plutarch, the Greek philosopher Anaxagoras lends to the sun's rays a subtle whistling that 'makes voices more discomfiting to hear during the day' than at night.

§ 8-12

Sun

                              sky

leper fills with

                              light

Scarlet flowers fill his mouth

-

sun   sky

flowers

                              eat night

leper   floats

                moon-like

                an infant grows

scarlet

                with sleep

-

all night
                        the moon cracks

and something slips out

-

leper

                    floats

over a field of eggs

like cries they flower
in place of light

-

mooon

My father recounts his childhood in Korea after the Korean War; the myth that lepers would kidnap children to eat in attempt to be cured.

15th century King Sungjong records an incident where a woman cut off her own finger, then dried and powdered it, and fed it to her husband upon hearing that human flesh was good for curing sickness; his leprosy was cured. This incident was read as an allegory of the wife's loyalty;

with the spread of Christian missionaries in Korea, the use of human flesh as medicine mutated into the image of lepers as child-eaters. Dispersed through the newly popularized printed public media, the discourse of infection and the hereditary nature of the disease started to emerge in propaganda supporting the sterilization and institutionalization of lepers after the 1930s. ——————— Eunjong Kim, Wagadu Vol. 4

Dodie Bellamy writes: "When the sick rule the world the limbs of the well will be chopped off in the middle of the night, the well one still alive, flailing and screaming. The limbs of the well will fetch exorbitant fees on the black market, sold to sorcerers who will dry the limbs and grind them into magic powders to be placed into amulets to ward off blindness and toxins. These amulets will bring prosperity to their owners."

Pharmakon: the poison and the cure.

§

—Do you believe that animals can feel pain? —I do believe that animals feel pain.

Some people, understanding that animals feel pain, take this as a basis to grant them rights. —Animals —At the lower threshold of the ability —The ability to feel or cognize pain —Many argue —Might not be subject to the same —Argument for rights —An argument which mostly comes down to the right not —Not to be consumed. —The privilege of the ability —The ability to feel pain

—There is the animal, who bellows in pain
—And there is the leper, whose disease slowly removes physical sensation

—Diana Hamilton, in her book *God Was Right*, writes: "I, an animal, am trying to tell you how I feel."

There is a popular critique of rights based on a Foucauldian framework. As Wendy Brown says, "Rights emblematize the ghostly sovereignty of the unemancipated individual in modernity." The problem of rights is that they extend the disciplinary power of the state to become a constitutive part of the construction of the citizen, as a "rights-bearing individual."

If one is to say that the treatment of lepers described is a violation of human rights, would one be trading in one version of the state's disciplinary power for another?

I do not know. I, an animal, am trying.

최 LINDSAY

Note: This project takes shape around a poem by modernist Korean poet 서정주 (Seo Jung-Joo), "문둥이" ("The Leper"):

해와 하늘 빛이
문둥이는 서러워

보리밭에 달 뜨면
애기 하나 먹고

꽃처럼 붉은 울음을 밤새 울었다

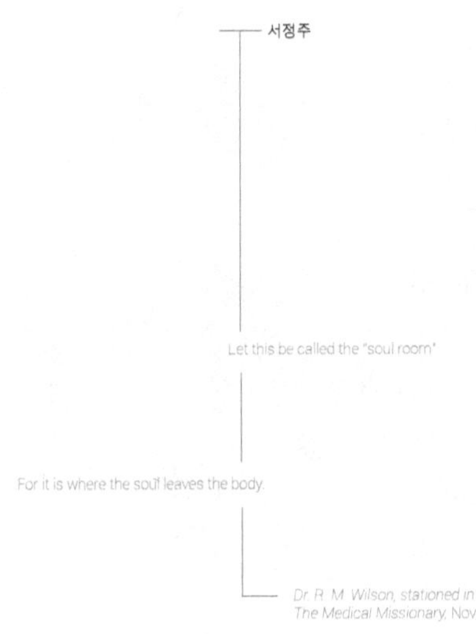

circus tent domed in new age

Kimberly Alidio

over Peking duck
a quick head jerk
can't eavesdrop
lack of tryhard

fascinates
scarification
a planeload
in from LA

certain harm done
whispers constant
processed capital
try make a sound

struggle under 100-lb
plate glass
bloodletter hilt is
a standing human

bathe in activated charcoal
our Olmec dragon

canceled Ansel
down on tasteful jade sun

brother seeks refund
for DNA results
100% circling one
pearl of the orient

dad calls a tall guy
My Bigoted Friend
his statement
signature jewelry

captive mountains
in three rings
sympathy
to crude truth

tweezed-off eyebrows
blank expression
of the tweezers'
gold alloy

godface
shrug
duh lack of
precise tool

at the Radnóti

Kimberly Alidio

I wanted to
lay my stomach
flat

against the
concrete floor
press

my cheek against
tercets
staggered and

descending
cry on glass a pool
that can't

form in the dirt
below
I desired

the poet's
re-interred force

keening

beauty
salvage our bodily
ground

account for
not those who died
for my

freedom
but at my
expense

My sovereignty steps
onto
the dead

breathing
destroys
in a very plain way

Transfusion via
our mouths
Carolee

Schneemann's Fuses
turned me on
even a penis

looks good in

heat maps
Snow doesn't

fall directly but
circles over
your head

imperceptibly
spirals my fingers
inside you

Will you fist me
if I beg in
a whisper

or without sound
subconsciously the way
you said I love you

a dozen times
before you said
it

A doorway unburied
fallen open
to the words

Locust Formation

Vidhu Aggarwal

Pressed into
    a garment

        so vocal I *I* am wired

    with voices
    the spiral voices
    of the locusts—

    the gyre
    of carnal It girls
    from every era

        a million circuits, a million

    thanks

        chords of statistics

rasp up my spine

through a field

of moving spines—thanks—

neck yanked forward—thanks, thanks

bare
seconds   jerk off, mouth open

current of mud and ash
I spit out

all the semen of the world, dust bunnies, rot

                              thanks thanks

Contributors

Vidhu Aggarwal's poetry and multimedia practices engage with world-building, video, and graphic media, and draw mythic schemas from popular culture and ancient texts. Her poetry book *The Trouble with Humpadori* (2016) imagines a cosmic mythological space for marginalized transnational subjects. Poems from *Humpadori* were listed in the top 25 from *Boston Review* in 2016 and appeared on Sundress Publications Best Poetry of 2016 list. *Avatara*, a chapbook from Portable Press at Yo-Yo Labs, is situated in a post-apocalyptic gaming world where A.I.s play at being gods. A Djerassi resident and Kundiman fellow, she teaches at Rollins College.

Kimberly Alidio is the author of *why letter ellipses* (selva oscura press, 2020), *: once teeth bones coral :* (Belladonna*, 2020), and *After projects the resound* (Black Radish Books, 2016). Her most recent chapbook is *a cell of falls* (Portable Press @ Yo-Yo Labs, 2019). Her work has been supported by the Jack Kerouac School of Disembodied Poetics, the Center for Art and Thought, and Kundiman. She holds a Ph.D. in History from the University of Michigan and an MFA candidacy in Poetry from the University of Arizona.

Amy Sara Carroll's books include *SECESSION* (Hyperbole Books, 2012), *FANNIE + FREDDIE/The Sentimentality of Post-9/11 Pornography*

(Fordham University Press, 2013), and *REMEX: Toward an Art History of the NAFTA Era* (University of Texas Press, 2017). Since 2008, she has been a member of Electronic Disturbance Theater 2.0, coproducing the *Transborder Immigrant Tool*. She coauthored *[({ })] The Desert Survival Series/La serie de sobrevivencia del desierto* (Office of Net Assessment/ University of Michigan Digital Environments Cluster Publishing Series, 2014). Published under a Creative Commons license, the volume has been digitally redistributed by CTheory Books (2015), CONACULTA E-Literatura/Centro de Cultura Digital (2016), and HemiPress (2017). Summer 2010 and every summer thereafter, Carroll has participated in the alternative arts space SOMA in Mexico City. She was a 2018-2019 Fellow in the University of Texas at Austin's Latino Research Initiative and a 2017-2018 Fellow in Cornell University's Society for the Humanities. Currently, she's an assistant professor of Literary Studies at The New School in New York City where she teaches literature and creative writing.

Youmna Chlala is an artist and a writer whose work investigates the relationship between fate and architecture through drawing, video, sculpture, prose and performance. She participated in the 33rd Bienal de São Paulo (2018), Lofoten Bienal (2017), Performa Biennial (2011) and has exhibited widely including at the Hayward Gallery, Rotterdam International Film Festival, The Drawing Center, Dubai Art Projects, Henie Onstad Kunstsenter, Camera Austria, ICA London, CultuurCentrum Bruges and Art In General. Her book of poetry *The Paper Camera* is forthcoming by Litmus Press. She is a Professor in the Humanities & Media Studies and Writing Departments at the Pratt Institute.

최 Lindsay is based in Berkeley California and is the author of *Transverse* (FuturePoem, 2020), and a chapbook, *Matrices* (Spect!

Books, 2017). They are a Kundiman Fellow and a Ph.D student in English Literature at UC Berkeley. More of their work can be found in *Omniverse, Amerarcana, Apogee, The Felt, Bettering American Poetry Vol. 2,* and elsewhere. Recent projects include a creative manuscript in and out of translation on the colonial history of leprosy in Korea.

Elisabeth Frost's books include *All of Us: Poems, Bindle* (in collaboration with artist Dianne Kornberg), and *The Feminist Avant-Garde in American Poetry*. She is Professor of English and Women's, Gender & Sexuality Studies at Fordham University, where she edits the Poets Out Loud Prize book series from Fordham Press.

Jamie Gray Gillette is from Jamestown, Rhode Island. She began writing for the *Newport Mercury Newspaper* in high school, but discovered a love for poetry through community workshops with Frequency Writers in Providence, RI, and at the Fine Arts Work Center in Provincetown, MA, where she later interned. She is currently in an undergraduate writing student at Bard College in New York.

raquel gutiérrez writes personal essays, memoir, art criticism, and poetry. A child of Mexican and Salvadoran immigrants, raquel was born and raised in Los Angeles and currently lives in Tucson, Arizona. She/they completed MFAs in Poetry and Non-Fiction from the University of Arizona. raquel runs the tiny press, Econo Textual Objects, which publishes works by QTPOC poets. Her/their poetry and essays have appeared in the *Los Angeles Review of Books, Open Space,* and elsewhere. Her/their first book, *Brown Neon* (Coffee House Press), will be published in the Spring 2021 and her/their first book of poetry, *Southwest Reconstruction* (Noemi Press), will be published in 2022.

Visual artist **Dianne Kornberg** has had more than thirty-five solo exhibitions in the United States and abroad, and her work is represented in the collections of multiple museums. She has been featured in a number of books including *Contemporary Art in the Northwest*. Her own books include *Field Notes* (2007), *India Tigers* (2009), *Madonna Comix* (2014, with poet Celia Bland), and *Bindle* (2015, with poet Elisabeth Frost). Kornberg is a Professor Emerita at Pacific Northwest College of Art in Portland, Oregon.

Saretta Morgan is the author of *Feeling Upon Arrival* (Ugly Duckling Presse, 2018) and *room for a counter interior* (Portable Press @ Yo-Yo Labs, 2017). She lives within the occupied Akimel O'odham territory of Phoenix, AZ where she teaches creative writing at Arizona State University and participates in the humanitarian efforts of No More Deaths Phoenix.

Christina Olivares is the author of *No Map of the Earth Includes Stars*, winner of the 2014 Marsh Hawk Press Book Prize, of the chaplet *Interrupt*, published by Belladonna* Series, and of *DSM/Partial Manual*, winner of the 2014 Vinyl 45 Chapbook Competition . She is the recipient of a 2015-2016 LMCC Workspace Residency, two Jerome Foundation Travel and Study Grants (2010 and 2014), a 2008 Teachers and Writers Fellowship, and has twice been nominated for a Pushcart Prize.

Aldrin Valdez is a Pinoy writer and visual artist. They grew up in Manila and Long Island and currently live in Brooklyn. Aldrin has been awarded fellowships from Queer/Art/Mentorship and Poets House. Their poetry & visual art appear in *The Felt*, *Femmescapes*, *Nat Brut*, *Poor Claudia*, and *The Recluse*. Aldrin has also presented work at Dixon Place, The Metropolitan Museum of Art, and The Poetry Project. Collaborating with writer & organizer Ted Kerr, Aldrin co-organized Foundational

Sharing (2011-2015), a salon series of readings, performances, & visual art. Most recently, they've co-curated two seasons of the Segue Reading Series with fellow poet Joël Díaz.

M.L. Vargas is a writer, educator and serves as poetry editor for *Aster(ix) Journal*. She was appointed poet in residence for the Montclair Art Museum (MAM) in 2014. Her work has appeared in various journals and anthologies, most recently *The Lake Rises: poems to & for our bodies of water*. She holds an MFA in poetry from Drew University and lives in New Jersey.